Hargrove

Group's

BIBLE SENSE™

1 PETER

STANDING FIRM IN JESUS

Group
Loveland, Colorado
www.group.com

Group resources actually work!

This Group resource incorporates our R.E.A.L. approach to ministry. It reinforces a growing friendship with Jesus, encourages long-term learning, and results in life transformation, because it's

Relational
Leaner-to-learner interaction enhances learning and builds Christian friendships.

Experiential
What learners experience through discussion and action sticks with them up to 9 times longer than what they simply hear or read.

Applicable
The aim of Chistian education is to equip learners to be both hearers and doers of God's Word.

Learner-based
Learners understand and retain more when the learning process takes into consideration how they learn best.

Group's BIBLESENSE™

1 PETER: STANDING FIRM IN JESUS
Copyright © 2007 Group Publishing, Inc.

Visit our Web site: **www.group.com**

Credits
Contributors: Jonathan Boggs, Kate S. Holburn, Joy-Elizabeth F. Lawrence, Keith Madsen, and Roxanne Wieman
Editor: Carl Simmons
Creative Development Editor: Matt Lockhart
Chief Creative Officer: Joani Schultz
Copy Editor: Dena Twinem
Art Director: Jean Bruns
Print Production Artist: Joyce Douglas
Cover Art Director: Jeff A. Storm
Cover Designer: Andrea Filer
Photographer: Rodney Stewart
Production Manager: DeAnne Lear

Library of Congress Cataloging-in-Publication Data
1 Peter : standing firm in Jesus. -- 1st American pbk. ed.
   p. cm. -- (Group's BibleSense)
   Includes bibliographical references.
   ISBN-13: 978-0-7644-3245-3 (pbk. : alk. paper)
1. Bible, N.T. Peter, 1st.--Textbooks. I. Group Publishing. II. Title: First Peter.
   BS2795.55.A12 2006
   227'.920071--dc22

                                        2006026946

10 9 8 7 6 5 4 3 2 1   16 15 14 13 12 11 10 09 08 07
Printed in the United States of America.

CONTENTS

CONTENTS
CONTINUED

INTRODUCTION
TO GROUP'S BIBLESENSE™

Welcome to **Group's BibleSense**™, a book-of-the-Bible series unlike any you've ever seen! This is a Bible study series in which you'll literally be able to *See, Hear, Smell, Taste, and Touch God's Word*—not only through seeing and hearing the actual book of the Bible you're studying on DVD, but also through thought-provoking questions and group activities. As you do these sessions, you'll bring the Word to life, bring your group closer together as a community, and help your group members to bring that life to others.

Whether you're new to small groups or have been doing them for years, you'll discover new, exciting, and—dare we say it—*fun* ways to learn and apply God's Word to your life in these sessions. And as you dig deeper into the Bible passage for each session and its meaning for your life, you'll find your life (and the lives around you) transformed more and more into Jesus' likeness.

Each session concludes with a series of opportunities on how to commit to reaching your world with the Bible passage you've just studied—whether it's in changing your own responses to others, reaching out to them individually or as an entire group, or by taking part in something bigger than your group.

So again, welcome to the world of BibleSense! We hope that you'll find the experiences and studies here both meaningful and memorable, and that as you do them together, your lives will grow even more into the likeness of our Lord, Jesus Christ.

—*Carl Simmons, Editor*

ABOUT THE SESSIONS

TASTE AND SEE (20 minutes)

Every BibleSense session begins with food—to give group members a chance to unwind and transition from a busy day and other preoccupations into the theme of the session. After the food and a few introductory questions, the group gets to experience Scripture in a fresh way. The passage for each session is included on DVD, as well as in print within the book. Also provided is "A Sense of History," a brief feature offering additional cultural and historical context.

DIGGING INTO SCRIPTURE (30 minutes)

This is the central part of the session. The group will have the chance to interact with the Scripture passage you've just read and watched, and, through questions and other sensory experiences, you'll learn how it applies to *your* life.

MAKING IT PERSONAL (15 minutes)

Now you'll move from understanding *how* the passage applies to your life, to thinking about ways you *can* apply it. In this part of the session, personal meaning is brought home through meaningful experiences and questions.

TOUCHING YOUR WORLD (25 minutes)

This is the "take home" part of the session. Each group member will choose a weekly challenge to directly apply this session's passage in a practical way in the week ahead, as well as share prayer requests and pray for one another. Also included is a "Taking It Home" section, with tips on how you can prepare for your next session.

GETTING CONNECTED

Pass your books around the room, and have everyone write his or her name, phone number, e-mail address, and birthday.

Name	Phone (H)	E-mail	Birthday
Montrell Spence	410-521-6523	PLOW3, MONH PAT @ COMCAST.NET	7/15/46
Pat Spence	(c)971 9437	" "	5/13/1955
Eardene Porter	4104055 3330	EARDene, Porter @ssa. gov	april 1
Theresa Bradshaw	410 363-8104	TJT Bradshaw @ hotmail.com	4/25
Marian Bland	(410)521-0915 (H)	mrbland@aol.com	3/8
Khadine Rajkumar	(917)583-1622	ka_creamofdcrop @ hotmail.com	04/14

SESSION 1:

FINDING JOY IN WAITING

1 PETER 1:1-12

In this session you'll discover how waiting prepares Christians for great rewards and joy, in this life and beyond.

PRE-SESSION CHECKLIST:

☐ **Leader:** Check out the Session 1 Leader Notes in the back of the book (page 81).

☐ **Food Coordinator:** If you are responsible for the Session 1 snack, see page 90.

☐ **Supplies:**

- 1 jigsaw puzzle (40-50 pieces)

- 1 seed (such as a sunflower seed) for each person in the group

TASTE AND SEE (20 minutes)

Your first session's snack is popcorn. You'll be doing the popping!

Break into subgroups of three to five, grab a bag, and take turns cooking your popcorn in the microwave. Wait until *everyone's* popcorn is done before you start eating.

While you're waiting, discuss the following:

• How good are you at waiting for something enjoyable? What kinds of things do you "like" to do while you wait?

Once all the popcorn has been popped, sit down and enjoy it together. And while you're doing that, discuss the following:

• Was the wait for the popcorn worth it? Why or why not?

• Did the smells coming out of the microwave help you in waiting, or does it make the waiting worse? Why?

 Watch the first chapter on the DVD (1 Peter 1:1-12). This passage can also be found on the following page.

1 Peter 1:1-12 (NLT)

¹This letter is from Peter, an apostle of Jesus Christ.

I am writing to God's chosen people who are living as foreigners in the provinces of Pontus, Galatia, Cappadocia, Asia, and Bithynia. ²God the Father knew you and chose you long ago, and his Spirit has made you holy. As a result, you have obeyed him and have been cleansed by the blood of Jesus Christ.

May God give you more and more grace and peace.

³All praise to God, the Father of our Lord Jesus Christ. It is by his great mercy that we have been born again, because God raised Jesus Christ from the dead. Now we live with great expectation, ⁴and we have a priceless inheritance—an inheritance that is kept in heaven for you, pure and undefiled, beyond the reach of change and decay. ⁵And through your faith, God is protecting you by his power until you receive this salvation, which is ready to be revealed on the last day for all to see.

⁶So be truly glad. There is wonderful joy ahead, even though you have to endure many trials for a little while. ⁷These trials will show that your faith is genuine. It is being tested as fire tests and purifies gold—though your faith is far more precious than mere gold. So when your faith remains strong through many trials, it will bring you much praise and glory and honor on the day when Jesus Christ is revealed to the whole world.

⁸You love him even though you have never seen him. Though you do not see him now, you trust him; and you rejoice with a

glorious, inexpressible joy. [9]The reward for trusting him will be the salvation of your souls.

[10]This salvation was something even the prophets wanted to know more about when they prophesied about this gracious salvation prepared for you. [11]They wondered what time or situation the Spirit of Christ within them was talking about when he told them in advance about Christ's suffering and his great glory afterward.

[12]They were told that their messages were not for themselves, but for you. And now this Good News has been announced to you by those who preached in the power of the Holy Sprit sent from heaven. It is all so wonderful that even the angels are eagerly watching these things happen.

DIGGING INTO SCRIPTURE (30 minutes)

As a group, discuss:

Tip: *To maximize participation, and also to have enough time to work through the session, at various points we recommend breaking into smaller subgroups of three or four.*

• What thoughts or emotions came to your mind while watching this session's Bible passage, whether just now or during the past week? *I thought about how God would eventually bring me through the trial I'm experiencing now*

Now break into subgroups.

Subgroup Leaders: Find a place where your subgroup can talk with few distractions. Plan to come back together in 10 minutes.

Read 1 Peter 1:1-12 and the following "A Sense of History" feature, and answer the questions that follow.

A SENSE OF HISTORY
...and a Sense of Expectancy

It is believed that the Apostle Peter wrote this letter between A.D. 62-64 to Christians in Asia Minor (modern-day Turkey). These Jesus-followers suffered trials and persecution because they would not participate in the worship of other gods. (For one example in Asia Minor, see Paul's clash with the Diana-worshippers of Ephesus in Acts 19:23-41.) Peter offers encouragement to a group of people who now lived as outcasts for a time but could look forward to Jesus' coming and an eternal inheritance.

Scholars believe that another of Peter's purposes for writing this letter was to reflect unity with Paul, who had been imprisoned in Rome by the Roman emperor Nero around this time. This show of support was especially important coming from Peter, one of the most impulsive and driven of Jesus' followers.

• Put yourself in the place of one of the early Christians receiving this letter from Peter, under these circumstances. How would you have reacted to Peter's words? What particular words or phrases jump out to you here?

There is wonderful joy ahead

• What does it mean to *you* that God chose you? How does knowing that God has an inheritance "kept in heaven for you, pure and undefiled, beyond the reach of change and decay" affect your day-to-day life? How else *should* it?

Come back together as a large group, and discuss any highlights from your subgroup discussion.

 Leader: Bring out your jigsaw puzzle—both your assembled pieces and your spare ones—and set it on the floor.

Gather around the puzzle, and discuss the following:

• What do you think the completed puzzle will look like? (Give as much detail as you can.) How easy or difficult is it for you to "see the big picture" of this puzzle right now?

Take turns picking up a missing piece and placing it into the puzzle. As you put your piece in, share about a time in your life you didn't see the "complete" picture of a good thing—a painful time that turned out great, or a promise you had to wait for, for example.

Once your group has completed the puzzle, take a few moments to admire your work. Then sit down and discuss the following questions:

Fun Fact: *Did you know that an elephant is pregnant for about 22 months before giving birth? Talk about a long period of expectancy!*

• Think about the stories you shared as you put your puzzle together. How did you handle waiting while those events were taking place? What or who helped you while you waited?

• What was it like when the pieces finally fell into place in those situations? How was that like or unlike the message Peter gives us in this passage?

MAKING IT PERSONAL (15 minutes)

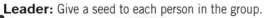

Leader: Give a seed to each person in the group.

Hold your seed tightly in one hand. As you do, discuss the following:

- What's one situation in your life right now that's like this seed—where you're still waiting to see what God is going to do with it? Explain.

> *"There, under the soil, unseen but very real, a transformation is going on...Waiting is the hardest part of the growth process. And for a seed, the waiting is done in the dark, in the black, cold, wet, airless underground."*
>
> —Luci Shaw, Water My Soul: Cultivating the Interior Life

Reread 1 Peter 1:8-12. Open your hand so that your seed is exposed to the light and lies in the palm of your hand, and discuss the following questions:

- Think again about the situation you discussed above. Which of God's promises in this passage can you apply to that situation? What do you think it would look like if you applied them?

- What's one thing you can do—or one person who can help you—to keep a Christlike perspective as you continue to wait for God to work in this situation?

TOUCHING YOUR WORLD (25 minutes)

Review the following "weekly challenge" options, and select the challenge you'd like to do. Turn to a partner, and share your choice. Then make plans to connect with your partner sometime between now and the next session to check in with and encourage one another.

☐ **KEEP A JOURNAL.** Think one more time about the situation you're struggling with or waiting for God's guidance in, and begin a regular journal of how God is addressing it. Write down your thoughts, feelings, and, most important, what you sense God is leading you to do—and *what* you do in response to that. Don't restrict yourself to just writing if you're on the more visually creative side—scribble, draw, paint. Whatever you do, focus on how God is working in your life through this situation, and thank him for it as you continue to work through it.

☐ **MAKE THE MOST OF YOUR WAIT.** Think about how you spend "anticipation time," then think of ways you can use it more wisely. Every time you find yourself waiting this week—such as in line, on hold, or in traffic—do something meaningful that will prevent impatience or irritation. Pray, make a list, or call a friend. Then apply those same principles to your faith. What's something valuable you can do as you wait, in whatever situation God has placed you in, for God's reward? Commit to doing it.

☐ **TALK TO GOD AS A GROUP.** If this has been a tough season for members of your group, set aside time this week to pray together as a group for the trials, hurts, or discouragement you've been experiencing. Ask God to give you strengthened hope and expectancy—and a deeper love for him that reflects in your joy and perseverance.

☐ **SHARE THE GOOD NEWS.** Get together with a non-Christian friend this week for coffee or lunch, and make a point of talking about your dreams and hopes—what each of you most looks forward to. Listen well, then share about your *greatest* anticipation, using 1 Peter 1:1-12 for inspiration. Talk about what it's like to look forward to heaven and eternal life with Jesus.

Come back together as a group. Share prayer requests, and then pray for everyone's needs. Let your Prayer Coordinator lead this time of prayer, especially for the situations you shared where you're still waiting or expecting.

Until next time...

Date _____

Time _____

Place _____

Taking It Home:

1. Set a goal for how many times you'll either read through or watch on your DVD the Session 2 Bible passage (1 Peter 1:13-25). Make a point to read the "Sense of History" feature in Session 2 (p. 22) before the next session. You may also want to review this week's passage as well—or even watch the entire book of 1 Peter straight through. (It takes about 20 minutes.) Let your weekly challenge partner know what goals you've set so he or she can encourage you and help hold you accountable.

2. Touch base sometime before the next session with your weekly challenge partner to compare notes on how you're both doing with the goals you've set.

3. If you volunteered for a role or signed up to help with food or supplies for the next session, be sure to prepare for this. The Session 2 supplies list can be found on page 18, and the Food Coordinator instructions are on page 90.

4. I commit to touching my world by learning to wait joyfully and expectantly in the following ways:

_____

_____

_____

_____

SESSION 2:

FOCUSING ON FOLLOWING

1 PETER 1:13-25

In this session you'll look at the qualities all Christians need to remain focused on as they follow Jesus.

PRE-SESSION CHECKLIST:

☐ **Leader:** Check out the Session 2 Leader Notes in the back of the book (page 82).

☐ **Food Coordinator:** If you are responsible for the Session 2 snack, see page 90.

☐ **Supplies:**

- A pen or pencil for each group member
- At least one item from today's culture for each subgroup, such as a cell phone, laptop computer, disposable coffee cup, gas container, running shoe, or credit or debit card

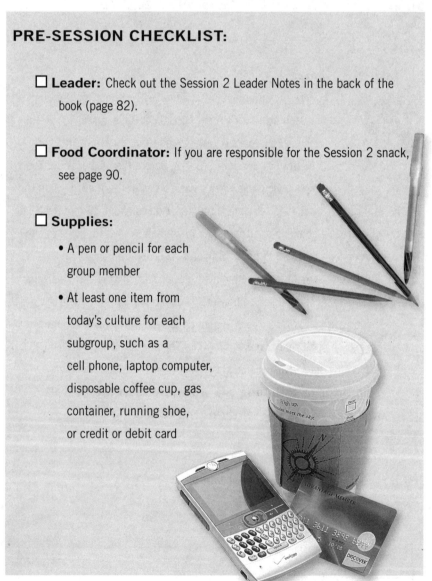

TASTE AND SEE (20 minutes)

Grab a bowl of ice cream—and while you're at it,
go wild with the toppings (or as wild
as you want to go, anyway)!

As you're enjoying your ice cream, discuss the following questions:

• What kinds of toppings did you put on your ice cream? Why?

• How do your toppings affect the taste of your ice cream? How would piling
on one particular topping have affected (or did affect) the taste differently?
(Be descriptive.)

• What's a situation going on in your life right now where you wish there was
more plain old "ice cream" and a few less "toppings"?

 Watch the second chapter on the DVD (1 Peter 1:13-25). This
passage can also be found on the following page if you would like to
follow along in your book.

1 Peter 1:13-25 (NLT)

[13]So think clearly and exercise self-control. Look forward to the gracious salvation that will come to you when Jesus Christ is revealed to the world. [14]So you must live as God's obedient children. Don't slip back into your old ways of living to satisfy your own desires. You didn't know any better then. [15]But now you must be holy in everything you do, just as God who chose you is holy. [16]For the Scriptures say, "You must be holy because I am holy."

[17]And remember that the heavenly Father to whom you pray has no favorites. He will judge or reward you according to what you do. So you must live in reverent fear of him during your time as "foreigners in the land." [18]For you know that God paid a ransom to save you from the empty life you inherited from your ancestors. And the ransom he paid was not mere gold or silver. [19]It was the precious blood of Christ, the sinless, spotless Lamb of God. [20]God chose him as your ransom long before the world began, but he has now revealed him to you in these last days.

[21]Through Christ you have come to trust in God. And you have placed your faith and hope in God because he raised Christ from the dead and gave him great glory.

[22]You were cleansed from your sins when you obeyed the truth, so now you must show sincere love to each other as brothers and sisters. Love each other deeply with all your heart.

23For you have been born again, but not to a life that will quickly end. Your new life will last forever because it comes from the eternal, living word of God. 24As the Scriptures say,

"People are like grass;
  their beauty is like a flower in the field.
The grass withers and the flower fades.
  25But the word of the Lord remains forever."

And that word is the Good News that was preached to you.

A SENSE OF HISTORY

A Different Kind of Hope

One of the most important themes of this passage—and this letter—is the hope that all Christians can have, regardless of circumstance. Set against the backdrop of persecution, the hope expressed by Peter here is even more striking. What did this hope look like in Peter's time, and why did it look so different from what the rest of the world had to offer? New Testament scholar N.T. Wright cites four elements of hope that were born out of early Christianity:

1) Vindication. During his life, Jesus spoke of the destruction of the Temple (Mark 13). The ultimate destruction of Herod's Temple in A.D. 70 demonstrated the truth of that prophecy as well as confirmed the triumph of Christ's death as the ultimate sacrifice for sins.

2) The offering of God's kingdom to the entire world. Hope for God's kingdom is hope for everyone in the world, in line with the Lord's Prayer, when Jesus said, "May your Kingdom come soon" (Matthew 6:9-13; Luke 11:2-4).

3) Physical resurrection after death. This hope contrasted greatly to contemporary mystery-religions and the nonphysical life-after-death beliefs of the Gnostics. To a society that believed in the purity of the soul amid the trappings of an earthly body, the idea of physical resurrection was revolutionary (Acts 17:16-34).

4) The personal return of Jesus. In Acts 1:11, followers of Jesus are told for the first time about Jesus' return. And today, we still joyfully await for Jesus to come again.

It was this kind of hope, in all its forms, that helped the early church to "[l]ook forward to the gracious salvation that will come to you when Jesus Christ is revealed to the world."

DIGGING INTO SCRIPTURE (30 minutes)

As a group, discuss:

• What thoughts or emotions came to your mind while watching this session's Bible passage, whether just now or during the past week?

Leader: Make sure everyone in the group has a pen or pencil.

> "Hope is definitely not the same thing as optimism. It is not the conviction that something will turn out well, but the certainty that something makes sense, regardless of how it turns out."
>
> —Václav Havel

Reread 1 Peter 1:13-25. As you do so, take your pencil or pen and mark up the text in this booklet, noting the four major themes in this passage with different symbols: hope (star), holiness/purity (triangle), fear of God (exclamation point), and love for neighbor (heart). When you've finished, discuss the following:

• What words or phrases did you highlight for each of these themes? Explain your choices. Why are each of these traits important in the life of a follower of Jesus?

• What dangers might there be in focusing on one of these over all the others? What's the danger in neglecting one or more of these?

• When have you seen these traits in others? Give examples. How do you think others have seen each of these traits in you?

Break up into subgroups.

Subgroup Leaders: Select one item from those the Leader has set out for your subgroup discussion. Give yourselves a maximum of 15 minutes for your subgroup discussion.

Pass your item around your subgroup. Think of the everyday uses for this object as you pass it around and look it over, then discuss the following questions:

• Think again about the four themes mentioned in this passage—hope, holiness, fear of God, and love for neighbor. How could your object symbolize one or more of these attributes?

• On the other hand, how might this object represent something that gets in the way of you following Jesus?

• What are some things you can do to help keep "things" in perspective—so that you can use them to help you *as* you follow Jesus rather than allowing them to distract you *from* that?

Come back together as a larger group. Put all your items back together in their original place, and share any highlights or questions from your subgroup discussion.

MAKING IT PERSONAL (15 minutes)

Reread 1 Peter 1:23-25, and answer the following questions:

• In what ways did the items you shared in your subgroup discussion remind you of this truth? What other evidence of this passage have you seen in your life?

• How is the kind of "glory" described here different from God's glory? How does knowing this help you keep your focus on living for Jesus?

• Which of the four attributes discussed in this session do you most need to develop in order to keep your spiritual focus in balance? What's one thing you can do to help develop it?

TOUCHING YOUR WORLD (25 minutes)

Review the following weekly challenge options, and select the challenge you'd like to do. Turn to a partner, and share your choice. Then make plans to connect with your partner sometime between now and the next session to check in and encourage one another.

☐ **PLANT A SEED.** Determine one aspect of your life (for example, a relationship or future plans) in which you need to have God's sense of hope. Plant a seed, and as you plant, pray that God will grow your hope as he will grow the seed. Place the pot in a place where you can see it, and pray for hope every time you see the pot.

☐ **THROW SOMETHING AWAY.** Today you looked at a specific item and talked about it in relation to following Jesus. Think about the things you own. Is there a specific item hindering you from holiness and walking with Jesus? Decide right now to throw the item away or donate it to charity. The item may not be bad in itself—nonetheless, it may be keeping you from following Jesus to the best of your ability.

☐ **REACH OUT TO A NEIGHBOR.** Think about the people who live in your neighborhood. Is there a neighbor you've never met or spent very little time getting to know? Do something intentional and kind for this neighbor this week: make bread, rake his or her lawn, deliver a potted plant, or simply stand on your driveway and chat. Do this joyfully, as a follower of Christ.

Come back together as a group. Share prayer requests, then pray for everyone's needs. As you share prayer requests, focus on ways you can better practice keeping your focus on Jesus as you follow him.

Until next time...

Date _____

Time _____

Place _____

Taking It Home:

1. Set a goal for how many times you'll either read through or watch on your DVD the Session 3 Bible passage (1 Peter 2:1-12). Make a point to read the "Sense of History" feature in Session 3 (p. 31) before the next session. You may also want to review this week's passage as well—or even watch the entire book of 1 Peter straight through. (It takes about 20 minutes.) Let your weekly challenge partner know what goals you've set so he or she can encourage you and help hold you accountable.

2. Touch base sometime before the next session with your weekly challenge partner to compare notes on how you're both doing with the goals you've set.

3. If you volunteered for a role or signed up to help with food or supplies for the next session, be sure to prepare for this. The Session 3 supplies list can be found on page 28, and the Food Coordinator instructions are on page 90.

4. I commit to touching my world this week by focusing on following Jesus in the following ways:

_____

_____

_____

SESSION 3:
PUTTING OUR STONES TOGETHER

1 PETER 2:1-12

In this session you'll explore how Christians are a part of *God's* house and how that can benefit both you and others.

PRE-SESSION CHECKLIST:

☐ **Leader:** Check out the Session 3 Leader Notes in the back of the book (page 83).

☐ **Food Coordinator:** If you are responsible for the Session 3 snack, see page 90.

☐ **Supplies:**

- 1 clear vase, half-filled with water

- Small or medium-sized stones—about a handful per person

TASTE AND SEE (20 minutes)

Break into subgroups.

Each subgroup should take one plate of fruit—no taking from another subgroup's plate! Get into your subgroups, and take whatever you like from your own plate. While you're eating, discuss the following questions.

- If you could have filled your group's plate with any one kind of fruit, what fruit would it have been? Why?

- What might happen if you restricted everyone to your own personal favorite fruit?

- What are some other reasons it might be important to have different kinds of fruit available?

Come back together as a large group, and discuss any highlights from your subgroup discussion.

Watch the third chapter on the DVD (1 Peter 2:1-12). This passage can also be found on the following page.

1 Peter 2:1-12 (NLT)

[1]So get rid of all evil behavior. Be done with all deceit, hypocrisy, jealousy, and all unkind speech. [2]Like newborn babies, you must crave pure spiritual milk so that you will grow into a full experience of salvation. Cry out for this nourishment, [3]now that you have had a taste of the Lord's kindness.

[4]You are coming to Christ, who is the living cornerstone of God's temple. He was rejected by people, but he was chosen by God for great honor.

[5]And you are living stones that God is building into his spiritual temple. What's more, you are his holy priests. Through the mediation of Jesus Christ, you offer spiritual sacrifices that please God. [6]As the Scriptures say,

> "I am placing a cornerstone in Jerusalem,
>> chosen for great honor,
> and anyone who trusts in him
>> will never be disgraced."

[7]Yes, you who trust him recognize the honor God has given him. But for those who reject him,

> "The stone that the builders rejected
>> has now become the cornerstone."
> [8]And,
> "He is the stone that makes people stumble,
>> the rock that makes them fall."

They stumble because they do not obey God's word, and so they meet the fate that was planned for them.

[9]But you are not like that, for you are a chosen people. You are royal priests, a holy nation, God's very own possession. As a result, you can show others the goodness of God, for he called you out of the darkness into his wonderful light.

[10]"Once you had no identity as a people;

now you are God's people.

Once you received no mercy;

now you have received God's mercy."

[11]Dear friends, I warn you as "temporary residents and foreigners" to keep away from worldly desires that wage war against your very souls. [12]Be careful to live properly among your unbelieving neighbors. Then even if they accuse you of doing wrong, they will see your honorable behavior, and they will give honor to God when he judges the world.

A SENSE OF HISTORY
Royal Priests, Then and Now

Peter's purpose in this passage was to remind the persecuted churches throughout Asia Minor that their identity was rooted in God's gracious choosing. Like the ancient tribe of Levi, they had been dubbed "his holy priests" (1 Peter 2:5). That phrase probably conjured up some very different images to Peter's original readers than it would to us today.

Beginning with Aaron, the tribe of Levi was called out from among the 12 tribes of Israel to serve in the tabernacle (Exodus 28:1-5). This small kin group was granted access to God's presence—a privilege shared with no other group in Israel or in the ancient world at large. But why the Levites? This was no doubt the question on the mind of every Israelite on the day of their election.

Levi, one of Jacob's 12 sons, was known for his cruelty; he and his brother Simeon had "murdered men, and...crippled oxen just for sport" (Genesis 49:6). On his deathbed, Jacob cursed the two tribes with perhaps the most devastating prophecy his sons could hear: "I will scatter them among the descendents of Jacob; I will disperse them throughout Israel" (Genesis 49:7). Truly, in the eyes of his father and brothers, Levi—and his line—deserved nothing.

But *God* chose the tribe of Levi. They would be his priests so all Israel would know that the honor of God's presence was not something earned, but a testimony to his great mercy. Nearness to God, from the first, was a gift.

God's plan for the Gentile Christians, then, was no different: He "chose things despised by the world, things counted as nothing at all, and used them to bring to nothing what the world considers important. As a result, no one can ever boast in the presence of God" (I Corinthians 1:28-29). Peter calls Christians to see themselves as they truly are—"God's very own possession" (verse 9)—a directive as important today as it ever was.

DIGGING INTO SCRIPTURE (30 minutes)

As a group, discuss:

- What thoughts or emotions came to your mind while watching this session's Bible passage, whether just now or during the past week?

 Leader: Set up the vase in the middle of the room, and give each subgroup enough stones for each subgroup member to have a small handful.

> ### In Other Words...
>
> In The Message, *Eugene Peterson paraphrases 1 Peter 2:5 this way:* "*Present yourselves as building stones for the construction of a sanctuary vibrant with life, in which you'll serve as holy priests offering Christ-approved lives up to God.*"

Subgroup Leaders: Find a place where your subgroup can talk with few distractions. Plan to come back together in 20 minutes.

Each subgroup member should pick up a handful of stones. Analyze each stone—feel its weight and texture. These stones will represent *your* contributions to your group's work.

Your task as a subgroup is to use your stones to create a three-dimensional figure in the shape of the vase in the middle of the room. Your model doesn't have to be the same size—just try to re-create the *shape*.

Now, start building!

Once you have as accurate a representation as possible, look around and see how other subgroups are doing. Staying in your subgroup, discuss the following questions:

- What were the biggest challenges to getting your vase built?

- Which stone was your "cornerstone"—the stone you used to anchor the rest of your "vase"? Why did you choose this particular stone?

If your rock vase is still standing, dismantle it and scatter the stones. Read 1 Peter 2:1-12, and discuss the following:

- Why do you think Peter calls Jesus the "living cornerstone"?

- With that in mind, what's the significance of Peter calling the members of the early church "living stones"?

- Peter reminds his readers that they were once like scattered stones: "Once you had no identity as a people; now you are God's people" (v. 10). In what ways have you experienced the difference between being an individual Christian and being a full-fledged citizen of God's people?

> **Did you know?**
> The cornerstone is far more than just the first slab of rock laid down. This stone determines every turn a building will take, securing both its stability and symmetry.

Return to the large group, and share highlights from your subgroup discussion.

Gather around the vase in the middle of the room. One by one, drop your stones into the vase's water, then discuss the following:

- How did this process differ from your first project? How were your feelings while doing it this way different?

- In what ways is letting the vase shape your stones together like the way Jesus shapes *us* together, as individual members of a community? How easy is it for you to let Jesus *do* that shaping? Give examples.

Stay gathered around the vase, and go on to "Making It Personal."

MAKING IT PERSONAL (15 minutes)

Read the passage from Ephesians in the margin, then answer the following questions:

> *"Always be humble and gentle. Be patient with each other, making allowance for each other's faults because of your love. Make every effort to keep yourselves united in the Spirit, binding yourselves together with peace. For there is one body and one Spirit, just as you have been called to one glorious hope for the future.*
>
> *However, he has given each one of us a special gift through the generosity of Christ. That is why the Scriptures say, 'When he ascended to the heights, he led a crowd of captives and gave gifts to his people.'"*
>
> —*Ephesians 4:2-4, 7-8*

• What's one area where you need to allow the Spirit to help you be more "humble and gentle...making allowance for each other's faults," and thus be more the kind of "living stone" Peter talks about?

• Re-read the last paragraph in the margin note. What "special gift" has God given you that enables you to uniquely contribute to God's house?

• Who in your group (or that you know elsewhere) has a "special gift" that corresponds with your "fault"— that is, who is strong in your area of weakness? What's one thing you can do to thank that person, or to draw from his or her strength, so you can help build God's house together?

TOUCHING YOUR WORLD (25 minutes)

Review the following weekly challenge options, and select the challenge you'd like to do. Turn to a partner, and share your choice. Then make plans to connect with your partner sometime between now and the next session to check in and encourage one another.

☐ **HELP EACH OTHER DEVELOP.** Remind your partner of the "special gift" he or she has been given, and pray together for the Spirit's help in developing it. Ask that God would enable both of you to more fully realize your gifts this week. You could even take time during your check-in this week to brainstorm creative new ways of utilizing your gifts.

☐ **A WORKING COMMUNITY.** This week, show a co-worker that he or she is not working alone. It could be something as simple as buying him or her a candy bar on your lunch break or something more, like offering to shoulder some of his or her workload in a stressful time. If you have someone in mind already, pray for him or her with your partner.

☐ **PUT YOUR STONES TOGETHER.** Offer to help your Outreach Coordinator plan a collective service project. Perhaps you could acquire a list of elderly men and women from your church and go on a lawn-mowing, leaf-raking, or snow-plowing expedition, or you might team up with an organization that actually *builds houses* for the needy!

Come back together as a group. Share prayer requests, then pray for everyone's needs. Ask God to tangibly remind you of both the privilege and the great responsibility of representing him to your neighbors. Also, take time to thank God for those whose strengths are different from yours, and ask God to show you ways to build each other up.

Until next time...

Date _____

Time _____

Place _____

Taking It Home:

1. Set a goal for how many times you'll either read through or watch on your DVD the Session 4 Bible passage (1 Peter 2:13–3:7). Make a point to read the "Sense of History" feature in Session 4 (p. 42) before the next session. Let your weekly challenge partner know what goals you've set so he or she can encourage you and help hold you accountable.

2. Touch base sometime before the next session with your weekly challenge partner to compare notes on how you're both doing with the goals you've set.

3. If you have volunteered for a role or signed up to help with food or supplies for the next session, be sure to prepare for this. The Session 4 supplies list can be found on page 38, and the Food Coordinator instructions are on page 90.

4. I commit to touching my world this week by learning to work together to show God's goodness in the following ways:

_____

_____

_____

_____

_____

SESSION 4:

FOLLOW THE LEADER...
JESUS' WAY

1 PETER 2:13–3:7

In this session you'll discover how honoring those in authority also honors and glorifies God.

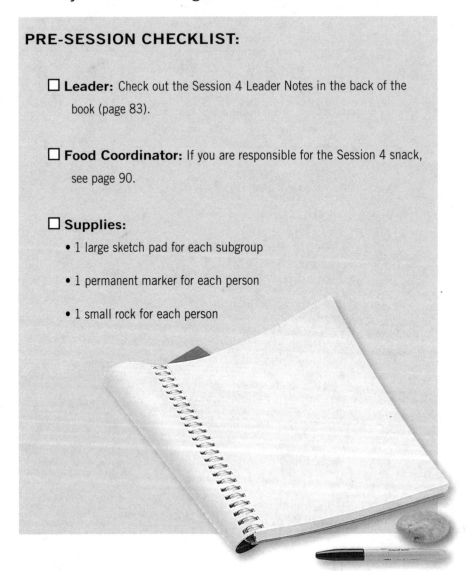

PRE-SESSION CHECKLIST:

☐ **Leader:** Check out the Session 4 Leader Notes in the back of the book (page 83).

☐ **Food Coordinator:** If you are responsible for the Session 4 snack, see page 90.

☐ **Supplies:**
- 1 large sketch pad for each subgroup
- 1 permanent marker for each person
- 1 small rock for each person

TASTE AND SEE (20 minutes)

Let your group eat cake! (Shortcake, that is.) As you enjoy your cake, discuss the following questions:

- Who would you describe as an honorable leader, past or present? What about that person do you feel makes (or made) him or her a great leader?

President Obama is honorable. I believe he has a gift to lead. He is able to get people's attention, encourage them to listen & believe in what he says, and I believe his intentions are sincere

- Who would you describe as a not-so-honorable leader—a corrupt leader, even? Why?

Hitler, he was evil, and he was able to get people to work for him to kill and torture others

- What emotions came to mind as you thought of your "honorable" leader? How about your not-so-honorable one? Why do you think these emotions came up in each case?

honorable - uplifting & positive
dishonorable - dark

Watch the fourth chapter on the DVD (1 Peter 2:13–3:7).

1 Peter 2:13–3:7 (NLT)

¹³For the Lord's sake, respect all human authority—whether the king as head of state, ¹⁴or the officials he has appointed. For the king has sent them to punish those who do wrong and to honor those who do right.

¹⁵It is God's will that your honorable lives should silence those ignorant people who make foolish accusations against you. ¹⁶For you are free, yet you are God's slaves, so don't use your freedom as an excuse to do evil. ¹⁷Repect everyone, and love your Christian brothers and sisters. Fear God, and respect the king.

¹⁸You who are slaves must accept the authority of your masters with all respect. Do what they tell you—not only if they are kind and reasonable, but even if they are cruel. ¹⁹For God is pleased with you when you do what you know is right and patiently endure unfair treatment. ²⁰Of course, you get no credit for being patient if you are beaten for doing wrong. But if you suffer for doing good and endure it patiently, God is pleased with you.

²¹For God called you to do good, even if it means suffering, just as Christ suffered for you. He is your example, and you must follow in his steps.

²²He never sinned,
      nor ever deceived anyone.
²³He did not retaliate when he was insulted,
      nor threaten revenge when he suffered.
He left his case in the hands of God,
      who always judges fairly.
²⁴He personally carried our sins
      in his body on the cross
so that we can be dead to sin
      and live for what is right.
By his wounds
      you are healed.

²⁵Once you were like sheep
who wandered away.
But now you have turned to your Shepherd,
the Guardian of your souls.

¹In the same way, you wives must accept the authority of your husbands. Then, even if some refuse to obey the Good News, your godly lives will speak to them without any words. They will be won over ²by observing your pure and reverent lives.

³Don't be concerned about the outward beauty of fancy hairstyles, expensive jewelry, or beautiful clothes. ⁴You should clothe yourselves instead with the beauty that comes from within, the unfading beauty of a gentle and quiet spirit, which is so precious to God. ⁵This is how the holy women of old made themselves beautiful. They trusted God and accepted the authority of their husbands. ⁶For instance, Sarah obeyed her husband, Abraham, and called him her master. You are her daughters when you do what is right without fear of what your husbands might do.

⁷In the same way, you husbands must give honor to your wives. Treat your wife with understanding as you live together. She may be weaker than you are, but she is your equal partner in God's gift of new life. Treat her as you should so your prayers will not be hindered.

A SENSE OF HISTORY

You Can't Be Serious?

It must have seemed like crazy talk! Many of these new Christians were Jewish, and the Jews were God's chosen race. They were not meant to serve *anyone*—let alone some pagan nation occupying *their* land. What was Peter thinking? How could he have honestly thought Christians—some Jewish, some Gentile, but almost all unfairly judged and ruled by the Romans—would just sit back and respect the Roman leadership?

Consider this:

In the Old Testament, Israel was ruled over by the Egyptians for 400 years (Genesis 15:12-16; Exodus 12:40-41). Later, when the Israelites rebelled against God, he sent Jeremiah to the people of Israel, telling them to submit to the Babylonian ruler, Nebuchadnezzar. But the people were more interested in what the false prophets, who promised the people that God would come and save them from occupation, said (Jeremiah 27). This refusal to listen to God and *his* prophets—and a constant attitude of rebellion against God and their rulers—led to most of the nation of Israel being taken captive to Babylon (2 Kings 24–25; 2 Chronicles 36).

The Jews were in captivity as a result of their own rebellion and sin against God—though they believed they were his people, they were stubbornly unable to trust him in the face of foreign rule. This attitude had not gone away at the time Peter wrote his epistle—when Jewish lands were occupied by Roman forces.

It may not have been easy for the early Christians to read Peter's words; but they revealed God's true heart for these new Christians: "It is God's will that your honorable lives should silence those ignorant people who make foolish accusations against you" (1 Peter 2:15). They were not to rebel with words and force, but to submit with respect and love. It was Peter's hope that their actions and lives would result, not in anger and violence, but in a fruitful witness and in fruitful lives—even the pagan ones of their occupiers—transformed for Jesus.

DIGGING INTO SCRIPTURE (30 minutes)

As a group, discuss:

• What thoughts or emotions came to your mind while watching this session's Bible passage, whether just now or during the past week?

Now break into subgroups.

Leader: Give each subgroup leader a large sketch pad and marker.

Subgroup Leaders: Use a maximum of 20 minutes for your discussion time. Before starting, quickly sketch a simple stick figure on the sketch pad.

We've read the comic strips, and watched the TV shows. We've all breathed a sigh of relief and thought: Thank goodness my boss isn't *that* bad...or *is* he (or she)? A bad boss can make life at work...well, not so great.

Imagine the worst possible boss. Pass around the sketch pad. Around your stick figure, write down whatever you think of when you think of a bad boss. Go ahead and shout out what you're writing as you put it down.

Once everyone's had a chance to write, discuss the following questions:

> **"** *The United States is a republic, and a republic is a state in which the people are the boss. That means us. And if the big shots in Washington don't do like we vote, we don't vote for them, by golly, no more.* **"**
> —Willis Goldbeck

Think about it!

How do we reconcile our responsibility to be informed and active citizens with our call as Christians to respect and honor those God has placed in leadership?

• When have you worked for an infuriatingly bad boss? What happened?

• How do you think God used you in (or despite) that situation?

As a group, read 1 Peter 2:22-25, and answer the following questions:
• Look at verse 23—what does it reveal about Jesus' trust in his heavenly Father?

• How can you personally trust God in the face of having to work for (or follow) someone who is not respectable, a bad leader, or even immoral?

• How do you think your submission could glorify God in such a situation?

Come back together as a larger group, and share any highlights or questions from your subgroup discussion.

MAKING IT PERSONAL (15 minutes)

Read 1 Peter 2:13–3:7. As you do so, think about which of these sections most challenge you, and which of these relationships are the most difficult for you to submit in.

Now break into pairs.

Leader: Give everyone a rock and a permanent marker.

On your rock, write down the name or initials of the person who came to mind most often as you were reading. Discuss the following questions with your partner (you can leave out names and personal details if you like):

• What makes it hard for you to respect and submit to this person?

• Why do you think God has put you in this relationship? How do you think God wants to use you to affect this person's life positively?

• What's one thing you can do to show God's love to this person through your lifestyle and actions in this coming week?

Come back together as a larger group, and share any highlights or questions from your pair-share discussions.

Put your rock in your pocket, and carry it around with you this week. Each time you feel it in your pocket, let it be a reminder to pray for that relationship and how God can use your submission for his glory.

TOUCHING YOUR WORLD (25 minutes)

Review the following weekly challenge options, and select the challenge you'd like to do. Turn to a partner, and share your choice. Then make plans to connect with your partner sometime between now and the next session to check in and encourage one another.

☐ **GIVE AN APPRECIATION GIFT.** Choose someone whose relationship is outlined in today's passages—a supervisor, leader, or spouse—and spend some time this week putting together an appreciation gift for that person. Compile lots of "favorite" things (his or her favorite snacks, a favorite movie, a gift certificate to a favorite store or restaurant), and include a card that expresses your appreciation for the person. Be sure to tell the person why you appreciate the relationship and his or her leadership.

☐ **PRAY EACH DAY.** Before you begin your day, pull out your rock from today's lesson and pray for your relationship with that person. Read the portion of today's Bible passage that pertains to your relationship. Ask God to help you live gracefully and respectfully in that relationship. Pray that you would see the best in that person, and always choose to give the benefit of the doubt. Seek God's wisdom in your daily interactions with that person, and trust that God can use your life as a witness to the person.

☐ **HONOR THE LEADERS IN YOUR COMMUNITY.** As a group, plan a dinner or dessert to honor one or two civic leaders in your community (for instance, city council or school board members). Plan the reception for a few months out, but be sure to send out invitations this week. You can also begin planning how you'll honor those leaders—maybe through community "thank you" speeches or through a fun night with games and other activities. There are lots of ideas for making the evening fun and rewarding for all involved!

Come back together as a group. Share prayer requests, then pray for everyone's needs. Pray that God would help each person in your group respect the people God has placed in authority in his or her life.

Until next time...

Date _____

Time _____

Place _____

Taking It Home:

1. Set a goal for how many times you'll either read through or watch on your DVD the Session 5 Bible passage (1 Peter 3:8-22). Make a point to read the "Sense of History" feature in Session 5 (p. 52) before the next session. Let your weekly challenge partner know what goals you've set so he or she can encourage you and help hold you accountable.

2. Touch base sometime before the next session with your weekly challenge partner to compare notes on how you're both doing with the goals you've set.

3. If you volunteered for a role or signed up to help with food or supplies for the next session, be sure to prepare for this. The Session 5 supplies list can be found on page 48, and the Food Coordinator instructions are on page 91.

4. I commit to touching my world this week by honoring those in authority in the following ways:

_____

_____

_____

_____

SESSION 5:

MAKING YOUR FAITH VISIBLE

1 PETER 3:8-22

In this session you'll discover the importance of both actions and words in sharing your faith.

PRE-SESSION CHECKLIST:

☐ **Leader:** Check out the Session 5 Leader Notes in the back of the book (page 84).

☐ **Food Coordinator:** If you are responsible for the Session 5 snack, see page 91.

☐ **Supplies:**
- 1 pitcher of water for each subgroup
- 1 water glass (empty) for each subgroup
- 1 bottle of food coloring for each subgroup
- An index card for each group member
- A pen or pencil for each group member

TASTE AND SEE (20 minutes)

Grab a couple of pieces of bread from different loafs. As you eat the bread, try to use your senses (taste, touch, smell, sight, even hearing—yes, you can share your guesses with one another) to identify what kind of bread each slice is.

Once your Food Coordinator has confirmed the identity of your breads, discuss the following questions together:

• What senses helped you to identify each kind of bread? In what ways?

• Which bread was the toughest to figure out? Why?

• So, what are some characteristics that help you figure out different kinds of *people*? their occupations? their temperaments?

Watch the fifth chapter on the DVD (1 Peter 3:8-22).

1 Peter 3:8-22 (NLT)

⁸Finally, all of you should be of one mind. Sympathize with each other. Love each other as brothers and sisters. Be tenderhearted, and keep a humble attitude. ⁹Don't repay evil for evil. Don't retaliate with insults when people insult you. Instead, pay them back with a blessing. That is what God has called you to do, and he will bless you for it. ¹⁰For the Scriptures say,

"If you want to enjoy life
   and see many happy days,
keep your tongue from speaking evil
   and your lips from telling lies.
¹¹Turn away from evil and do good.
   Search for peace, and work to maintain it.
¹²The eyes of the Lord watch over those who do right,
   and his ears are open to their prayers.
But the Lord turns his face
   against those who do evil."

¹³Now, who will want to harm you if you are eager to do good? ¹⁴But even if you suffer for doing what is right, God will reward you for it. So don't worry or be afraid of their threats. ¹⁵Instead, you must worship Christ as Lord of your life. And if someone asks about your Christian hope, always be ready to explain it. ¹⁶But do this in a gentle and respectful way. Keep your conscience clear. Then if people speak against you, they will be ashamed when they see what a good life you live because you belong to Christ. ¹⁷Remember, it is better to suffer for doing good, if that is what God wants, than to suffer for doing wrong!

¹⁸Christ suffered for our sins once for all time. He never sinned, but he died for sinners to bring you safely home to God. He suffered physical death, but he was raised to life in the Spirit.

¹⁹So he went and preached to the spirits in prison—²⁰those who disobeyed God long ago when God waited patiently while Noah was building his boat. Only eight people were saved from drowning in that terrible flood. ²¹And that water is a picture of baptism, which now saves you, not by removing dirt from your body, but as a response to God from a clean conscience. It is effective because of the resurrection of Jesus Christ.

²²Now Christ has gone to heaven. He is seated in the place of honor next to God, and all the angels and authorities and powers accept his authority.

A SENSE OF HISTORY
Some Tough Texts

First Peter 3:8-22 has historically been one of the most confounding texts in Christian theology—particularly because of verses 19-21. Noah? Spirits in prison? The flood? Baptism? Really, what does it all mean? Even as prominent a figure as Martin Luther couldn't quite figure it out, saying in essence, "I don't know what Peter means here."

So what are the existing theories on these verses? Here are a few:

• St. Augustine proposed that Jesus preached through Noah to the people who were alive then. Colossians 1:16-17 and 1 Corinthians 10:4 support that Christ has always been actively involved in this world.

• Another theory is that after Jesus died and before he rose again, he preached to those who were dead physically and spiritually—specifically, those who had lived during Noah's time.

• Again, between his death and resurrection, Christ descended into hell and declared his victory to the spirits there. Genesis 6, 2 Peter 2, and Jude 6 are texts used to support this view.

That's a few of the theories out there. So, what does it have to do with Peter's ultimate message? In this case, it has to do with suffering for the cause of righteousness. Jesus suffered for us all in his death, knowing his ultimate goal was our salvation. Noah suffered for God, knowing his ultimate goal was eternity in the presence of God. The people of Noah's time, however, gave up their eternal promises for the instant gratification of earthly ones. We are called, like Noah—like Jesus—to endure whatever suffering comes on this earth for the promise of eternity in God's presence.

DIGGING INTO SCRIPTURE (30 minutes)

As a group, discuss:

• What thoughts or emotions came to your mind while watching this session's Bible passage, whether just now or during the past week?

Now break into subgroups.

Leader: Give each Subgroup Leader a pitcher of water, an empty water glass, and a bottle of food coloring.

Subgroup Leaders: Use a maximum of 20 minutes for your discussion time.

Read 1 Peter 3:8-12, then discuss the following:

• Think about the breads you tried earlier. Some things make them immediately recognizable. By the same token, what attributes of Christians should make them immediately—and always—recognizable?

Set up the pitcher of water, cups, and food coloring on a table or on the floor. One by one, describe a time in word or deed when you gained a positive impression of a Christian (or Christianity) through your contact with that person. As you talk about it, pour a little bit of water from the pitcher into the glass.

Now, describe a time when you had a bad interaction with a Christian—when your contact with that person left a bad taste in your mouth and affected your view of Christians...and Christianity. This time, as you describe your experience, put a small drop of food coloring in your glass.

Once everyone has taken turns, discuss the following questions:

• How do you think people's negative interactions with Christians color their view of Christians and Christianity as a whole?

• Which do you think affects people more—a positive experience or a negative one?

• Do you think this cup of water and food coloring is an accurate metaphor for how positive and negative interactions with Christians affect people's views of Christianity? Why or why not?

Read 1 Peter 3:13-17, and answer the following questions:

• Describe a time when someone *asked* you about your faith in Jesus. What do you think prompted that person to ask you?

• How has your attitude in the face of suffering reflected your trust in Jesus? How do you think people around you perceived that attitude?

• What are some ways that you can counteract the negative impressions others have of Christians and/or Christianity?

> *"Preach the gospel at all times and when necessary use words."*
> —*St. Francis of Assisi*

Come back together as a larger group, and share any highlights or questions from your subgroup discussion.

MAKING IT PERSONAL (15 minutes)

Leader: Give everyone in the group an index card, and make sure everyone has a pen or pencil.

On one side of your index cards, write down at least one Christlike attribute you want to live out every day (if you need ideas, look back at 1 Peter 3:8-12 or at 1 Corinthians 13:1-7). Think of the loaves of bread—how can people *recognize* you as a Christian through your lifestyle and actions? How is God challenging you personally?

When you've finished, flip the card over. On this side, take time to write down why you believe in Jesus. Seriously—define the hope that you have (1 Peter 3:15). What does it mean to you? Why is it precious to you? Why should others want what you have? Don't worry about writing down the perfect answer right now—but start thinking about it, and write down your best answer. What would you say if someone asked you to explain your hope in Jesus Christ?

Find a partner, and share your insights with one another. Then discuss the following questions together:

- If you didn't label yourself as a Christian, do you think people would be able to identify you as one? Why or why not?

- Look at both sides of your card. What connections do you see between the attributes you want to develop and what you believe about Jesus? What other connections do you think *should* be there?

- What's one way that you can successfully combine your actions and words in the coming week, to make your faith in Jesus visible to others?

Keep your cards with you this week as a reminder to put the desires of your heart together with your actions, so others can see Jesus in you.

Staying in your pairs, go directly to "Touching Your World."

TOUCHING YOUR WORLD (25 minutes)

Review the following weekly challenge options, and select the challenge you'd like to do. Turn to a partner, and share your choice. Then make plans to connect with your partner sometime between now and the next session to check in and encourage one another.

☐ **LISTEN.** Practice your listening skills this week. Don't do it with a motive in mind—do it because you want to build relationships. It's a method Jesus often used: He listened to people's stories and to their hearts, and knew their pain and therefore knew how God specifically could help them. Listen to people's stories; ask them questions about their lives; pray for them as well.

☐ **CONSIDER YOUR NEIGHBORS.** Make a list of your neighbors, whether they're geographical neighbors or people you see frequently. How are you impacting them for Jesus? Think through recent interactions you've had with them—were they positive or negative? Did you share your hope—either through words or actions? Now, consider specific ways you can reflect Christ's hope to one or two of them this week. Invite someone over for dinner. Fix a broken lawnmower. Smile at the cashier in your grocery store and ask how he or she is doing. You could even...well, what's something you *could* do?

☐ **SERVE YOUR COMMUNITY TOGETHER.** As a group, find a way to show your love and hope through your actions. Plan a simple service project for your community. For example, you could hand out bottles of water in the park on a hot day, walk through your neighborhood and pick up trash, or go to your neighbors and offer a window-washing service. Read 1 Corinthians 13:4, and remember to do your service in love—and if someone asks you why you're doing it, be prepared to give an answer!

Come back together as a group. Share prayer requests, then pray for everyone's needs. Pray that God would help each person in your group live out his or her faith in both action and word.

Until next time...

Date _____

Time _____

Place _____

Taking It Home:

1. Set a goal for how many times you'll either read through or watch on your DVD the Session 6 Bible passage (1 Peter 4:1-19). Make a point to read the "Sense of History" feature in Session 6 (p. 62) before the next session. Let your weekly challenge partner know what goals you've set so he or she can encourage you and help hold you accountable.

2. Touch base sometime before the next session with your weekly challenge partner to compare notes on how you're both doing with the goals you've set.

3. If you volunteered for a role or signed up to help with food or supplies for the next session, be sure to prepare for this. The Session 6 supplies list can be found on page 58, and the Food Coordinator instructions are on page 91.

4. **I commit to touching my world this week by sharing my faith through words and actions in the following ways:**

_____

_____

_____

_____

SESSION 6 :

STANDING TOGETHER IN TRIAL

1 PETER 4:1-19

In this session you'll discuss how God's gifts can help both us and others in times of trial.

PRE-SESSION CHECKLIST:

☐ **Leader:** Check out the Session 6 Leader Notes in the back of the book (page 85).

☐ **Food Coordinator:** If you are responsible for the Session 6 snack, see page 91.

☐ **Supplies:**
- 1 gift catalog or advertising supplement focused on gift ideas per subgroup
- 1 gift-package bow for everyone in the group

TASTE AND SEE (20 minutes)

Warning! Some varieties of our nachos will be *very* spicy! Take a sample of each one. On the sheet of paper next to each one, rate the sample on spiciness from "1" (totally wimpy) to "10" (a fiery ordeal).

After rating each sample, choose which one(s) you like best, and fill your plate. As you eat, share your answers to the following questions:

• What kinds of spicy foods did your family eat when you were growing up? Who was the boldest in trying them? What do you think the appeal is of food that can make your eyes water, your throat burn, and your nose run?

• OK—so what's the appeal of *experiences* that test your abilities to endure them?

• What's one experience that tested you but was still enjoyable? How is it different sharing about that experience with others who've had similar experiences, rather than with those who haven't?

Watch the sixth chapter on the DVD (1 Peter 4:1-19).

1 Peter 4:1-19 (NLT)

[1]So then, since Christ suffered physical pain, you must arm yourselves with the same attitude he had, and be ready to suffer, too. For if you have suffered physically for Christ, you have finished with sin. [2]You won't spend the rest of your lives chasing your own desires, but you will be anxious to do the will of God. [3]You have had enough in the past of the evil things that godless people enjoy—their immorality and lust, their feasting and drunkenness and wild parties, and their terrible worship of idols.

[4]Of course, your former friends are surprised when you no longer plunge into the flood of wild and destructive things they do. So they slander you. [5]But remember that they will have to face God, who will judge everyone, both the living and the dead. [6]That is why the Good News was preached to those who are now dead—so although they were destined to die like all people, they now live forever with God in the Spirit.

[7]The end of the world is coming soon. Therefore, be earnest and disciplined in your prayers. [8]Most important of all, continue to show deep love for each other, for love covers a multitude of sins. [9]Cheerfully share your home with those who need a meal or a place to stay.

[10]God has given each of you a gift from his great variety of spiritual gifts. Use them well to serve one another. [11]Do you have the gift of speaking? Then speak as though God himself were speaking through you. Do you have the gift of helping others? Do it with all the strength and energy that God supplies. Then everything you do will bring glory to God through Jesus Christ. All glory and power to him forever and ever! Amen.

¹²Dear friends, don't be surprised at the fiery trials you are going through, as if something strange were happening to you. ¹³Instead, be very glad—for these trials make you partners with Christ in his suffering, so that you will have the wonderful joy of seeing his glory when it is revealed to all the world.

¹⁴So be happy when you are insulted for being a Christian, for then the glorious Spirit of God rests upon you. ¹⁵If you suffer, however, it must not be for murder, stealing, making trouble, or prying into other people's affairs. ¹⁶But it is no shame to suffer for being a Christian. Praise God for the privilege of being called by his name! ¹⁷For the time has come for judgment, and it must begin with God's household. And if judgment begins with us, what terrible fate awaits those who have never obeyed God's Good News? ¹⁸And also,

> "If the righteous are barely saved,
>   what will happen to godless sinners?"

¹⁹So if you are suffering in a manner that pleases God, keep on doing what is right, and trust your lives to the God who created you, for he will never fail you.

A SENSE OF HISTORY

Fiery Trials in the Early Church

From the beginning, followers of Jesus have gone through difficult times. Peter denied his Lord because he feared suffering the same fate Christ suffered (Matthew 26:69-75), and the disciples huddled behind locked doors after the crucifixion because they feared the Jewish leaders (John 20:19). Indeed, in those times Christians were under threat from two sources: Jewish authorities and the forces of Rome. The former were more of a factor early, but as time went on, Rome became the predominant threat.

Jewish leaders persecuted Christians because they saw them as guilty of blasphemy against God. The martyrdom of Stephen (Acts 6:8–7:60) began "a great wave of persecution" (Acts 8:1) which scattered the disciples throughout Judea and Samaria. Jewish religious leadership was also instrumental in encouraging King Herod to kill James the brother of John (Acts 12:1-5), and eventually encouraging the arrest and execution of Paul (Acts 21:26-36).

Roman authorities became more and more involved in persecution of Christians because they saw them as a threat to their political authority and as undermining their religion. Both Jesus and Paul were accused of undermining Caesar (Luke 23:1-2; Acts 17:5-7). Because of the suspicion against Christians, Nero tried to frame them for the burning of Rome and so initiate an intense persecution of Christians in Rome that saw them thrown to lions and burned as human torches in Nero's gardens. It is most likely that both Paul and Peter were martyred during this time.

DIGGING INTO SCRIPTURE

As a group, discuss:

• What thoughts or emotions came to your mind while watching this session's Bible passage, whether just now or during the past week?

Now break into subgroups.

Leader: Give each subgroup a gift catalog or advertising supplement.

Subgroup leaders: Find a place where your subgroup can talk with few distractions. Plan to come back together in 20 minutes.

Take a minute or two to pass around your catalog or advertising supplement. Look through it together, then discuss the following questions:

• What kinds of gifts are featured in your publication? What are the "selling points"— the qualities that are emphasized with the expectation that people would value them?

> "*But all the endeavors of men, all the emperor's largesse and the propitiations of the gods, did not suffice to allay the scandal or banish the belief that the fire had been ordered. And so...Nero set up as the culprits and punished with the utmost refinement of cruelty a class hated for their abominations, who are commonly called Christians.*"
>
> —*Tacitus,* Annales *XV. 44 (c. A.D. 115)*

• If someone from a different world were to look at this catalog or supplement, what do you think it would say to them about our culture?

Read 1 Peter 4:7-13, and answer the following questions:

• If you were to create a catalog for the gifts *Peter* is writing about, what pictures might you include? What are some "selling points" for each gift?

• What are some different ways that these gifts can be used? How are they important during a time of trial or testing, such as Peter's readers were facing?

• If Peter were to be transported to our own time, what gifts do you think he would say are most needed for the trials or challenges we face as a society today? Why?

> **"**If God hadn't put me on earth mainly to stroke tennis balls, he certainly hadn't put me here to be greedy. I wanted to make a difference, however small, in the world, and I wanted to do so in a useful and honorable way.**"**
>
> —*Arthur Ashe*

Come back together as a larger group, and share any highlights or questions from your subgroup discussion.

MAKING IT PERSONAL (15 minutes)

Now break into pairs.

Leader: Give a gift-package bow to each person in the group.

Look around the room. What do you see that might symbolize a gift you'd like to give to your partner? For instance, a clock might symbolize giving the gift of time, because your partner always seems pressed for time. Or you might see a light and use it as a symbol of the enlightenment you'd like him or her to have for a problem he or she is struggling with.

Identify your symbolic gift, then take your bow and put it on that item. Present the gift to your partner—if it's physically possible to do so—and explain why you chose that item. (Of course, all items remain the property of your Host!)

After your presentations, discuss the following in your pairs:

• What reaction did you have to the gift you received? How great would it be if you really had what this gift represents? Explain.

• In what ways is the thing or idea your gift represents like the spiritual gifts Peter talks about in this session's passage? How is it different?

• What's one gift you *do* already have from God? How can you apply that gift in your current situation, or to help someone else going through a tough time right now?

Come back together as a larger group, and discuss any highlights from your pair-share time.

Take the bows off your gifts, and keep them as a reminder of how God has already equipped you for whatever situation he has put each of you in—and how God will continue to equip you for the trials ahead.

TOUCHING YOUR WORLD (25 minutes)

Review the following weekly challenge options, and select the challenge you'd like to do. Get with your partner, and share your choice. Then make plans to connect with your partner sometime between now and the next session to check in and encourage one another.

☐ **EXPLORE YOUR GIFTS.** Talk with your pastor or another church leader. Ask what gifts he or she sees in you. Ask your friends as well. Or take a spiritual gifts inventory; many are available online at sites such as www.churchvolunteercentral.com or www.churchgrowth.org. Explore other biblical passages on spiritual gifts, such as Romans 12:6-8; 1 Corinthians 12:7-31; and Ephesians 4:7-16. If you already have some idea of your gifts, discover new ways they can be used to help others going through trials. For instance, if you discover you have a gift for teaching, explore the possibility of using that gift to tutor underprivileged youth.

☐ **GO ON A FAST.** This means of identifying with the suffering of Jesus has a long historical tradition. Jesus himself fasted in the wilderness (Matthew 4:2), as did the church at Antioch before sending out Barnabas and Paul on their first missionary journey (Acts 13:2). Fasting also helps a person get in touch with the suffering of the poor and hungry. Fast for a meal, a day...or longer. Think about giving the money you save by not eating to a hunger-relief organization.

☐ **SUPPORT SOMEONE GOING THROUGH A TIME OF TRIAL.** Perhaps you know someone going through a trial that you've gone through yourself. Give that person a call or spend some time with him or her. Listen to his or her feelings and experiences—how is it like what you went through, and how is it different? How did God meet *you* in that situation? What did you learn that might help this person? Let him or her suggest a way you can help, and follow through with the suggestion the best you know how.

Come back together as a group. Share prayer requests, then pray for everyone's needs. Pray especially that your group can effectively support each other in the midst of your struggles.

Until next time...

Date _____

Time _____

Place _____

Taking It Home:

1. Set a goal for how many times you'll either read through or watch on your DVD the Session 7 Bible passage (1 Peter 5:1-14). Make a point to read the "Sense of History" feature in Session 7 (p. 72) before the next session. You may also want to review this week's passage as well—or even watch the entire book of 1 Peter straight through. (It takes about 20 minutes.) Let your weekly challenge partner know what goals you've set so he or she can encourage you and help hold you accountable.

2. Touch base sometime before the next session with your weekly challenge partner to compare notes on how you're both doing with the goals you've set.

3. If you volunteered for a role or signed up to help with food or supplies for the next session, be sure to prepare for this. The Session 7 supplies list can be found on page 68, and the Food Coordinator instructions are on page 91.

4. **I commit to touching my world this week by using my gifts to help deal with trials—mine *and* others'—in the following ways:**

_____

_____

_____

_____

SESSION 7:

BUILDING AS A TEAM

1 PETER 5:1-14

In this session you'll discuss how both leading and following are needed to build God's kingdom.

PRE-SESSION CHECKLIST:

☐ **Leader:** Check out the Session 7 Leader Notes in the back of the book (page 85).

☐ **Food Coordinator:** If you are responsible for the Session 7 snack, see page 91.

☐ **Supplies:**

- A 1-foot square piece of cardboard for each subgroup

- 1 small glue bottle (preferably quick-drying) for each subgroup

- 1 package of craft sticks (150 per package) for each subgroup

TASTE AND SEE (20 minutes)

For our snack today you have a choice: a "flock of wings" or a "flock of Peeps." Take as many as you like of one or the other, but *no combos!*

Once you've made your choices: All those who chose wings should sit in one subgroup; all those who chose Peeps should sit in a separate subgroup. As you eat, discuss the following questions:

• Why did you choose the one snack over the other?

• Look around your subgroup. What qualities would you say typify your "snack flock" over those who chose the other option?

• If someone (outside of your Subgroup Leader, of course) were to lead your particular subgroup, what advice would you give them?

 Watch the final chapter on the DVD (1 Peter 5:1-14).

1 Peter 5:1-14 (NLT)

[1]And now, a word to you who are elders in the churches. I, too, am an elder and a witness to the sufferings of Christ. And I, too, will share in his glory when he is revealed to the whole world. As a fellow elder, I appeal to you: [2]Care for the flock that God has entrusted to you. Watch over it willingly, not grudgingly—not for what you will get out of it, but because you are eager to serve God. [3]Don't lord it over the people assigned to your care, but lead them by your own good example. [4]And when the Great Shepherd appears, you will receive a crown of never-ending glory and honor.

[5]In the same way, you younger men must accept the authority of the elders. And all of you, serve each other in humility, for

"God opposes the proud
   but favors the humble."

[6]So humble yourselves under the mighty power of God, and at the right time he will lift you up in honor. [7]Give all your worries and cares to God, for he cares about you.

[8] Stay alert! Watch out for your great enemy, the devil. He prowls around like a roaring lion, looking for someone to devour. [9]Stand firm against him, and be strong in your faith. Remember that your Christian brothers and sisters all over the world are going through the same kind of suffering you are.

[10]In his kindness God called you to share in his eternal glory by means of Christ Jesus. So after you have suffered a little while, he will restore, support, and strengthen you, and he will place you on a firm foundation. [11]All power to him forever! Amen.

[12]I have written and sent this short letter to you with the help of Silas, whom I commend to you as a faithful brother. My purpose in writing is to encourage you and assure you that what you are experiencing is truly part of God's grace for you. Stand firm in this grace.

[13]Your sister church here in Babylon sends you greetings, and so does my son Mark. [14]Greet each other with Christian love.

Peace be with all of you who are in Christ.

A SENSE OF HISTORY
The "Babylonian Connection"

Peter refers to "your sister church here in Babylon" in verse 13, but was there actually a church in Babylon at this time? It's not totally out of the question. Babylon was the country where the people of Judah had been taken in captivity to in 586 B.C. It was one of the most devastating experiences of their national history. In time, however, some adapted to this foreign land, so that when the Jews were finally allowed to return to their own country, some chose to stay. In time Babylon became a center of Jewish scholarship; the Jewish historian Josephus even issued a special edition of his histories for them.

It's much more likely, however, that Peter was referring to the church at Rome. *Babylon* was regularly used as a code name for Rome by both Jews and Christians. In the book of Revelation, the name is almost certainly used to represent Rome, which was portrayed as being "drunk" with the blood of the saints and martyrs (Revelation 17–18). It was natural to refer to Rome as "Babylon" because so much of what the nation had suffered in Babylon, Christians and Jews were now suffering at the hands of Rome. The Roman Empire even destroyed the Temple and the city of Jerusalem in a similar manner in A.D. 70.

There was most certainly a church at Rome, and Peter is strongly connected to the church by tradition. Peter's reference to "your sister church here in Babylon" is a not-so-subtle reminder to Peter's readers that he (as well as the Roman church) lived in the hotbed of persecution. Therefore, he could write with understanding about having faith in the midst of such persecution.

Peter himself was believed to have been executed in Rome by being crucified upside down around A.D. 64.

DIGGING INTO SCRIPTURE (30 minutes)

As a group, discuss:

• What thoughts or emotions came to your mind while watching this session's Bible passage, whether just now or during the past week?

Now break into subgroups.

Leader: Give each subgroup a 1-foot square piece of cardboard, a glue bottle, and a package of craft sticks.

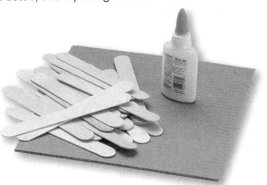

Subgroup Leaders: Find a place where your subgroup can work around a table and talk with few distractions. Plan to come back together in 20 minutes.

Each subgroup is to construct any kind of building they want out of craft sticks. The only requirement is that there be a cross somewhere in the structure. Designate a "construction supervisor"—someone who will direct your subgroup *and* have final authority over the design and construction of your building.

Take about seven or eight minutes to work. Afterward, take a minute to look over your building, as well as those made by the other subgroups. Then come back to your own subgroup to discuss the following:

• How well do you think your subgroup worked together on this project?

• How well did you respond to the instructions of your "construction supervisor"? What did he or she do that helped the subgroup? What, if anything, could he or she have done to help the subgroup more?

> "*Everyone wants to lead; no one wants to be a servant. We would rather be generals than privates...But to be like Jesus is to be a servant. That's what he called himself.*"
>
> —Rick Warren, The Purpose Driven Life

Read 1 Peter 5:1-14, and answer the following questions:
• Discuss a time you've seen or known of when both leaders and followers have shown humility in a situation. What did that look like? What made it so different from situations where humility wasn't being shown?

• Why is it important for Christian leaders to show a "good example" rather than "lord it over" those under their authority?

• What does your own church or group need to do to provide the kind of leadership (and support) that would help members "stand firm" in times of stress? Give some positive examples of what that would look like.

Come back together as a larger group, and share any highlights or questions from your subgroup discussion.

MAKING IT PERSONAL (15 minutes)

Reread 1 Peter 5:1-4. Then discuss the following:

• In what areas of life—such as home, work, or friendship—do you feel like you've done a good job leading "by your own good example"?

• How have you seen others in this group lead by their examples? Give some examples of your own.

• Where do you think God may be calling you to be more of a "leader" right now? What do you feel you need in order to do that?

> **"*If I only had a little humility, I'd be perfect.*"**
> —*Ted Turner*

• How can this group support you as you take the next step toward becoming what God has called you to become in that area?

TOUCHING YOUR WORLD (25 minutes)

Review the following weekly challenge options, and select the challenge you'd like to do. Get with your partner, and share your choice. Then make plans to connect with your partner sometime during the next week to check in and encourage one another.

☐ **FOCUS ON "WALKING YOUR TALK."** In what areas have you, in all honesty, done a better job talking about than actually doing? Most of us fall into this trap at least occasionally—telling teenagers to do what you haven't done well yourself, or putting a standard on those working under you that you haven't demonstrated yourself. Focus on those areas in the coming week, and commit yourself to "lead them by your own good example."

☐ **LEARN TO SUBMIT TO AUTHORITY.** Submitting to authority is not only biblical, but an essential part of working on a team. Yet many of us have "issues" with authority. Talk to a trusted friend about your struggle with authority and where the roots of it might lay. Pray each morning for a spirit of humility—not to be a doormat or "yes person," but a servant of God.

☐ **PARTICIPATE IN CHRISTIAN LEADERSHIP TRAINING.** If Christian leaders are to lead by example, then we need to learn those examples ourselves. Many churches host regular workshops in "servant leadership," including Stephen Ministry (www.stephenministries.org) and Church Growth, Inc. (www.churchgrowth.net). Ask your pastor about participating in such training, and recruit other Christians to join you.

☐ **HELP BUILD A NEW MINISTRY.** Oftentimes people are seeking to build new ministries, such as to feed the hungry, provide positive activities for youth, or care for the elderly. Make an appointment to talk to your pastor about what's in the works, and join the team that best matches your gifts and concerns.

Come back together as a group. Share prayer requests, then pray for everyone's needs. Pray especially that God will keep all of you "on a firm foundation" in the weeks to come.

Leader: If you haven't already, take some time to discuss what's next for the group. Will you stay together and work on another BibleSense book? Will you celebrate your time together with a party and be done? Or will you have a party, *then* start another BibleSense book the following week?

Touch-Base Time:

Set a date, time, and place to get together with your weekly challenge partner in the next week.

Date _____

Time _____

Place _____

Taking It Home:

1. Touch base during the week with your weekly challenge partner to compare notes on how you're both doing with the goals you've set.

2. You may want to review this week's passage—or even watch the entire book of 1 Peter straight through on your DVD, now that you've finished your study. (It takes about 20 minutes to watch the entire book.)

3. **I commit to touching my world this week by improving my ability to lead *and* to follow in the following ways:**

_____

_____

_____

_____

NOTES & ROLES

CONTENTS

LEADER NOTES

GROUP ROLES

LEADER NOTES

GENERAL LEADER TIPS

1. Although these sessions are designed to require minimum advance preparation, try to read over each session ahead of time and watch the DVD chapter for that session. Highlight any questions you feel are especially important for your group to spend time on during the session.

2. Prior to the first session, watch the Leading a BibleSense™ Session overview on the DVD. You'll notice that this isn't your average Bible study. Food? Activities? Don't forget that Jesus used food and everyday items and experiences in *his* small group all the time. Jesus' disciples certainly weren't comfortable when he washed their feet (John 13:4-17), and were even a bit confused at first. Jesus reassured them, "You don't understand now what I am doing, but someday you will" (verse 7), and it turned out to be a powerful lesson that stayed with them the rest of their lives. It's our prayer that your group will have similar experiences.

3. Take the time to read the group roles on pages 87-88, and make sure all critical tasks and roles are covered for each session. The three roles you *absolutely need filled* for each session are Leader, Host, and Food Coordinator. These roles can be rotated around the group, if you like.

4. Discuss as a group how to handle child care—not only because it can be a sensitive subject, but to give your group an opportunity to begin working together *as* a group. See the Child Care Coordinator tips on page 95 for ideas on how to handle this important issue.

5. Don't be afraid to ask for volunteers. Who knows—they may want to commit to a role once they've tried it (and if it's available on a regular basis). However, give people the option of "no thanks" as well.

6. Every session will begin with a snack, so work closely with your Food Coordinator—he or she has a vital role in each session. If you need to, go ahead and ask for donations from your group for the snacks that are provided each week.

7. Always start on time. If you do this from Session 1, you'll avoid the group arriving and starting later and later as the study goes on.

8. Be ready and willing to pray at times other than the closing time. Start each session with prayer—let everyone know they're getting "down to business." Be open to other times where prayer is appropriate, such as when someone answers a question and ends up expressing pain or grief over a situation he or she is currently struggling with. Don't save it for the end—stop and pray right there and then. Your Prayer Coordinator can take the lead in these situations, if you like, but give him or her "permission" to do so.

9. Try not to have the first or last word on every question (or even most of them). Give everyone the opportunity to participate. At the same time, don't put anyone on the spot—remind group members that they can pass on any questions they're not comfortable answering.

10. Keep things on track. There are suggested time limits for each section. Encourage good discussion, but don't be afraid to "rope 'em back in." If you do decide to spend extra time on a question or activity, consider skipping or spending less time on a later question or activity so you can stay on schedule.

11. Don't let your group off the hook with the assignments in the "Touching Your World" section—this is when group members get to apply in a personal way what they've learned. Encourage group members to follow through on their assignments. You may even want to make it a point to ask how they did with their weekly challenges during snack time at the beginning of your next session.

12. Also note that the last weekly challenge in "Touching Your World" is often an outreach assignment that can be done either individually or as a group. Make sure that group members who take on these challenges are encouraged and, if it's a group activity, organized. If your group has an Outreach Coordinator, let him or her take the lead here, and touch base regularly.

13. Lastly, the single most important thing a leader can do for his or her group is to spend time in prayer for group members. Why not take a minute and pray for your group right now?

Session 1 Leader Notes

1. Read the General Leader Tips starting on page 79, if you haven't already. Take a peek at the tips for other group roles as well (pp. 87-88).

2. Make sure everyone has a BibleSense book and DVD. Have the group pass around their books to record contact information (p. 7) before or during "Taste and See" or at the end of the session.

3. If this is the first time you're meeting as a group, you may want to take a few minutes before your session to lay down some ground rules. Here are three simple ones:

- Don't say anything that will embarrass anyone or violate someone's trust.
- Likewise, anything shared in the group *stays* in the group, unless the person sharing it says otherwise.
- No one has to answer a question he or she is uncomfortable answering.

4. Take time to review the group roles on pages 87-88 before you get together, and be ready to discuss them at the end of your session. Assign as many roles as you can, but don't pressure anyone to take on something he or she doesn't want or isn't yet sure about.

5. For this session, you're responsible for the items in the Supplies list on page 8. You'll want to assign the Supplies list for future sessions; the Host is the most sensible choice to handle this responsibility, or it can be rotated around the group.

6. Regarding the items in this session's Supplies list: Set out a partially assembled puzzle of about 40-50 pieces that is a picture of something recognizable, such as a mountain scene or a well-known painting. (A children's floor puzzle, with *big* pieces, would be ideal.) Keep your puzzle box and partially assembled puzzle hidden until it's time to set the puzzle out during "Digging Into Scripture" so group members won't be able to figure it out too quickly. Keep the extra pieces turned over when you bring them in. At the same time, try to have as many pieces assembled as you can (without giving away the picture), so your activity can keep moving along.

Try not to spend more than 10 minutes on the actual activity, if possible. If you have a smaller group and/or a couple dozen pieces out of the puzzle, feel free to change up the activity so that each group member has to put in two or three pieces at a time while telling his or her story.

7. Likewise, note the seeds in your Supplies list and their usage in "Making It Personal." Whatever kind of seeds you use, make sure they're the growable kind, rather than just edible seeds. **Extra Impact:** Consider providing special laser-imprinted seeds that produce leaves with patterns and writing. (One location you can find these unique seeds for purchase is www.magicbeans.us.) They cost a bit more than other seeds but will make a tremendous impact on your group and be a powerful, memorable takeaway. If you can't get these beans in time for your first session, they still would make a great gift for your group members during or at the end of this study.

8. Unless you're ahead of the game and already have a Food Coordinator, you're responsible for the snack for this first session. You'll want to make sure you have a Food Coordinator for future sessions, but for this session, be sure to review the Food Coordinator assignment on page 90.

9. Before you dismiss this first session, make a special point to remind group members of the importance of following through on the weekly challenge each of them has committed to in the "Touching Your World" section.

Session 2 Leader Notes

1. If new people join the group this session, use part of the "Taste and See" time to ask them to introduce themselves to the group, and have the group pass around their books to record contact information (p. 7). Give a brief summary of the points covered in Session 1.

2. If you told the group during the first session that you'd be following up to see how they did with their "Touching Your World" commitment, be sure to do so. This is an opportunity to establish an environment of accountability. However, be prepared to share how you did with your *own* commitment from the first session.

3. See the marking-up activity at the beginning of "Digging Into Scripture." Decide before your session whether you'll have the group read the passage to themselves or whether you'll ask someone to read it aloud.

4. Note also the Supplies list, and the activity in "Digging Into Scripture." Set these items in one place to the side before your group gathers; it's OK if they see them beforehand, but don't draw attention to them until it's time to do this activity. If you decide to use a gas container, make sure it's empty and clean on the outside (and reasonably clean on the inside). You don't want to get anyone's clothes or carpet dirty or overwhelm them with smells. Likewise, if you use a credit card, make sure it's an expired one—or one of those fake samples that come in the mail.

5. For the closing prayer time, ask for volunteers to pray for requests that were shared. You may want to ask the Prayer Coordinator in advance, if you have one, to lead the prayer time. If you don't have a Prayer Coordinator and decide to lead the prayer time yourself, look over the Prayer Coordinator tips on page 94, and keep them in mind as you lead the time. If you ask someone else to lead, try to ask the person—and direct him or her to these tips—in advance. Also, if your group has decided to use a prayer list, make sure you use it during your prayer time.

Session 3 Leader Notes

1. Are you praying for your group members regularly? It's the most important thing a leader can do for his or her group. Take some time now to pray for your group, if you haven't already.

2. Note the Supplies list, and the activity in "Digging Into Scripture." Try to find a vase with a curve or two to it—don't make it impossible to copy, but don't make it easy, either. Challenge your group, and have a good laugh if things don't go exactly as planned. If it's really difficult to locate a clear vase, you can substitute an opaque one—but clear is better.

Session 4 Leader Notes

1. Congratulations! You're halfway through this study. It's time for a checkup: How's the group going? What's worked well so far? What might you consider changing as you approach the remaining sessions?

2. On that note, you may find it helpful to make some notes right after your session to help you evaluate how things are going. Ask yourself, "Did everyone participate?" and "Is there anyone I need to make a special effort to follow up with before the next session?"

3. Note the discussion questions in "Taste and See," and be prepared. Not everyone in your group is always going to agree on everything. So if any of your conversations today turn into political ones, remind everyone to slow down, take a deep breath, and listen. Political conversations aren't necessarily bad—and can turn into wonderful opportunities to get to know each other better and to consider a different viewpoint. Respect your friends, listen to their insights—and, if things get a little heated, remind your group of the point of today's session (to glorify God by respecting authority).

4. Note the Supplies list, and the activity in "Making It Personal." This rock will need to be a little larger than last week's stones—large enough for group members to write initials on.

5. For the reading in "Making It Personal," decide in advance whether you'll have one person read, take turns, or have group members read the passage silently. It's a fairly long passage, but it covers a number of different relationships—including ones that several of your group members may be struggling with currently.

Session 5 Leader Notes

1. Remember the importance of starting and ending on time, and remind your group of it, too, if you need to.

2. Look over the Supplies list and the sensory experience in "Digging Into Scripture." Decide in advance whether you'll have subgroups put their materials on tables or on the floor. You may want to keep towels available, in either case (and just in case).

3. For some great ideas on how to share the love of Jesus with others—or, to paraphrase St. Francis, preach the gospel without words—check out *Irresistible Evangelism* by Steve Sjogren, Dave Ping, and Doug Pollock (Group Publishing). Anyone interested in serving free hot dogs at the mall?

4. This also would be a good time remind group members of the importance of following through on the weekly challenge each of them have committed to in "Touching Your World."

Session 6 Leader Notes

1. How are you doing with your prayer time for the group? Take some time to pray for your group now, if you haven't done so already.

2. Since your next session will be your group's last one in this book, you may want to start discussing with the group what to do after you've completed this study.

3. On that note, you may want to do another group checkup before you begin your next study (if that's the plan). Ask yourself, "Is everyone participating?" and "Is there anyone I need to make a special effort to follow up with?"

4. Note the activity in "Making It Personal." Let your Host know in advance to keep some easily transportable (and less breakable) things available around the room (in other words, don't clean *too* much this week). Also let your Host know that bows could be placed on their items, so if there are some things they really don't want bows stuck to, let you (and the group) know.

For this activity, if partners get stuck for "gift ideas," encourage them to share situations where they could really use a little help right now. Also, remind them to take care that the "gifts" they present each other are to be affirming, not patronizing or potentially insulting (even if meant in good humor).

Session 7 Leader Notes

1. Since this is your group's last session in this book, make sure you have a plan for next week...and beyond.

2. As part of this last session, you may want to consider having people share, either during the "Taste and See" section or at the end of your session, what this study or group has meant to them. This can also be incorporated into the beginning of your prayer time, if you like.

3. Note the Supplies list, and the sensory experience during "Digging Into Scripture." Try to have a table available for each subgroup; if that's not possible, locate other flat surfaces (like an uncarpeted floor) where subgroups can work.

4. Here's one suggestion for making the closing prayer time for this last session special: Have the group form a prayer circle. Then have each person or couple, if comfortable doing so, take a turn standing or kneeling in the middle of the circle while the group prays specifically for them. Your Prayer Coordinator is a good candidate to lead this.

5. Another prayer suggestion: Have group members open and extend their hands as they pray, and literally "hand" their concerns over to God. Then likewise, draw their hands back in, as they "receive" back from God in prayer.

GROUP ROLES

ROLE DESCRIPTIONS

Review the group roles that follow.

We have provided multiple roles to encourage maximum participation. At minimum, there are three roles that we recommend be filled for every session— Leader, Food Coordinator, and Host. These particular roles can also be rotated around the group, if you like. Other roles (Outreach and Inreach Coordinators, especially) are best handled by one person, as they involve tasks that may take more than one week to accomplish. It's *your* group—you decide what works best. What's most important is that you work together in deciding.

Not everyone will want to take on a role, so no pressure. But as you come to own a role in your group, you'll feel more connected. You'll even become more comfortable with that role you're not so sure you want to volunteer for right now.

Read through the following roles together, and write in each volunteer's name after his or her role in your book, so everyone remembers who's who (and what roles may still be available):

LEADER _____.

Your session Leader will facilitate each session, keeping discussions and activities on track. If a role hasn't yet been filled or the person who normally has a certain role misses a session, the session Leader will also make sure that all tasks and supplies are covered.

FOOD COORDINATOR _____.

The Food Coordinator will oversee the snacks for each group meeting. This role not only builds the fellowship of the group, but it is an especially important role for this particular study since specific snacks are assigned for each session and are used to lead group members into the meaning of each session.

HOST _____.

Your Host will open up his or her home and help group members and visitors feel *at* home. It sounds simple enough, but the gift of hospitality is critical to your group. If group members don't feel welcome, chances are they won't stay group members for long. Your Host should also be responsible for supplying—or locating someone who *can* supply—the items in the Supplies list at the beginning of each session. (They're usually common household items, so don't panic.)

OUTREACH COORDINATOR _____.

Different sessions often highlight different ways to reach out—sharing the Word, extending personal invitations to others to come to your group, or participating in service projects where your group meets the needs of those in your neighborhood or community. Your Outreach Coordinator will champion and coordinate those efforts to reach outside of your group.

GROUP CARE ("INREACH") COORDINATOR _____
_____. Everyone needs a pat on the back once in a while. Therefore, every group also needs a good Inreach Coordinator— someone who oversees caring for the personal needs of group members. That might involve coordinating meals for group members who are sick, making contact with those who have missed group, arranging for birthday/anniversary celebrations for group members, or sending "just thinking of you" notes.

PRAYER COORDINATOR _____.

Your Prayer Coordinator will record and circulate prayer requests to the rest of the group during the week, as well as channel any urgent prayer requests to the group that may come up during the week. He or she may also be asked to lead the group in prayer at the close of a session.

SUBGROUP LEADER(S) _____

_____.

To maximize participation, and also to have enough time to work through the session, at various points we recommend breaking into smaller subgroups of three or four. Therefore, you'll need Subgroup Leaders. This is also a great opportunity to develop leaders within the group (who could possibly lead new groups in the future).

CHILD CARE COORDINATOR _____.

Your Child Care Coordinator will make arrangements to ensure that children are cared for while their parents meet, either at the Host's house or at some other agreed-upon location(s). Depending on the makeup of your group, this could be a make-or-break role in ensuring you have a healthy group.

Again, if you don't have volunteers for every role (aside from Leader, Food Coordinator, and Host), that's OK. You may need to think about it first or become more comfortable before making a commitment. What's important is that once you commit to a role, you keep that commitment. If you know you'll miss a session, give the session Leader as much advance notice as possible so your role can be covered.

Whether you volunteer for a role now or want to think things over, take time before the next session to look over the "Group Role Tips" section that begins on the following page. You'll find plenty of useful ideas that will help your group and your role in it (or the role you're considering) be the best it can be.

GROUP ROLE TIPS

FOOD COORDINATOR

1. Sometimes your snack will be a surprise to the rest of the group. Be sure to work closely with your Host and Leader so the timing of your snacks helps this session be the best it can be.

2. You may also need to arrive a few minutes early to set up the surprise. Set up a time with the Host for your arrival before the meeting.

FOOD COORDINATOR ASSIGNMENTS AND IDEAS

Session 1

The snack for your first session is an easy one—bags of microwave popcorn. You don't even have to pop them! That's going to be part of the session, so just have the bags ready. Plan for one bag for every three to five people in your group.

Session 2

For this session, offer your group ice cream—and a *wide* variety of toppings. Include cherries, hot fudge, nuts, sprinkles, marshmallows, or anything else you can think of. The most important thing is to make sure there's different kinds of *toppings*—not just different kinds of sweet stuff.

Session 3

Create assorted mixed-fruit plates for this session—one for each subgroup. Have different combinations of fruit on each plate, so different plates have the potential to appeal to different subgroups.

Session 4

Prepare a pineapple-and-strawberry shortcake for everyone in your group. Purchase individual-sized shortcakes at your local grocery store as well as a pineapple (or canned pineapple rings) and strawberries. Cut the pineapple into rings, then place a ring on top of each shortcake. In the center of each pineapple ring, place a strawberry. For extra flavor, sprinkle the whole thing with shredded coconut.

Session 5

Prepare or purchase several loaves of bread—each with a different flavor, such as banana bread, rye bread, and zucchini bread. Before the small group time, slice each loaf and place the slices on platters. Be sure you don't label the breads or leave any evidence of packaging near the breads—people need to guess what kinds of breads they're eating!

Session 6

For this session, provide several different combinations of nachos, including choices with mild salsa, medium salsa, and hot salsa. You could even add fresh jalapeño (or habanero!) peppers to your dishes. Also, place a piece of paper next to each dish—group members will be rating the spiciness of each. Consider it a challenge! And mix up the plates. Don't just go from mild to hot—surprise your group. If someone's stomach is particularly sensitive, a little extra guidance is OK (just don't tell anyone else).

Session 7

For your last session's snack, provide the following two options: Buffalo chicken wings and Peeps (you know—the marshmallow treats shaped like baby chicks that sell like crazy every Easter). Have plenty of both available, as group members will only get to choose from one of the two options (at least until your "Taste and See" time is over).

Thanks again for all your work in making this a successful study!

HOST

1. Before your group gets together, make sure the environment for your session is just right. Is the temperature in your home or meeting place comfortable? Is there enough lighting? Are there enough chairs for everyone? Can they be arranged in a way that everyone's included? Is your bathroom clean and "stocked"? Your home doesn't need to win any awards—just don't let anything be a distraction from your time together.

2. Once your session's started, do what you can to keep it from being interrupted. When possible, don't answer the phone. Ask people to turn off their cell phones or pagers, if necessary. If your phone number's an emergency contact for someone in the group, designate a specific person to answer the phone so your session can continue to run smoothly.

3. If you're responsible for the supplies for your study, be sure to read through the Supplies list before each session. If there's any difficulty in supplying any of the materials, let your Leader know or contact someone else in the group who you know has them. The items required for each session are usually common household items, so most weeks this will be pretty easy. Make sure everything's set up before the group arrives.

4. Be sure also to check out what the Food Coordinator's got planned each week. Sometimes the snack is a surprise, so he or she may need your help in *keeping* it a surprise from the rest of the group. Your Food Coordinator may also need to arrive a few minutes early to set up, so be sure to work out a time for his or her arrival before the meeting.

5. And, of course, make your guests feel welcome. That's your number-one priority as Host. Greet group members at the door, and make them feel at home from the moment they enter. Spend a few minutes talking with them after your session—let them know you see them as people and not just "group members." Thank them for coming as they leave.

OUTREACH COORDINATOR

1. Don't forget: New people are the lifeblood of a group. They will keep things from getting stale and will keep your group outwardly focused—as it should be. Encourage the group to invite others.

2. Don't overlook the power of a personal invitation—even to those who don't know Jesus. Invite people from work or your neighborhood to your group, and encourage other group members to do the same.

3. Take special note of the "Touching Your World" section at the end of each session. The last weekly challenge is often an "outreach" assignment that can be done either individually or as a group. Be sure to encourage and follow up with group members who take on these challenges.

4. If group members choose an "outreach" option for their weekly challenge, use part of your closing time together to ask God for help in selecting the right service opportunity and that God would bless your group's efforts. Then spend some time afterward discussing what you'll do next.

5. Consider having an event before you begin your BibleSense study (or after you finish it). Give a "no obligation" invite to Christians and non-Christians alike, just to have the opportunity to meet the others in your group. Do mention, however, what the group will be studying next, so they have an opportunity to consider joining you for your next study. Speak with your Leader before making any plans, however.

6. As part of your personal prayer time, pray that God would bring new people to the group. Make this a regular part of your group's prayer time as well.

GROUP CARE ("INREACH") COORDINATOR

1. Make a point of finding out more about your group members each week. You should be doing this as a group member, but in your role as Inreach Coordinator, you'll have additional opportunities to use what you learn to better care for those in your group.

2. If a group member has special needs, be sure to contact him or her during the week. If it's something the group can help with, get permission first, then bring the rest of the group into this ministry opportunity.

3. Find out the special dates in your group members' lives, such as birthdays or anniversaries. Make or bring cards for other group members to sign in advance.

4. If someone in your group is sick, has a baby, or faces some other kind of emergency, you may want to coordinate meals for that person with the rest of the group.

PRAYER COORDINATOR

1. Pray for your group throughout the week, and encourage group members to pray for one another. Keep a prayer list, and try to send out prayer reminders after each session.

2. Be sure to keep your group up to date on any current or earlier prayer requests. Pass on "praise reports" when you have them. Remind them that God not only hears, but *answers*, prayer.

3. Remember that the role is called Prayer *Coordinator*, not "Official Pray-er for the Group" (whether that's what your group would prefer or not). At the same time, some members of your group may be uncomfortable praying aloud. If there are several people in your group who don't mind praying, one person could open your prayer time and another close it, allowing others to add prayers in between. Give everyone who wants to pray the opportunity to do so.

4. Prayers don't have to be complex, and probably shouldn't be. Jesus himself said, "When you pray, don't babble on and on as people of other religions do. They think their prayers are answered merely by repeating their words again and again" (Matthew 6:7).

5. If some group members are intimidated by prayer, begin prayer time by inviting group members to complete a sentence as he or she prays. For example, ask everyone to finish the following: "Lord, I want to thank you for…"

6. Don't overlook the power of silent prayer. Don't automatically fill "dead spaces" in your prayer time—God may be trying to do that by speaking into that silence. You might even consider closing a session with a time of silent prayer.

SUBGROUP LEADER(S)

1. These sessions are designed to require a minimum of preparation. Nonetheless, be sure to read over each session and watch the DVD in advance, to get comfortable with those sections where you may be responsible for leading a subgroup discussion. Highlight any questions you think are important for your subgroup to spend time on during the next session.

2. Try not to have the first or last word on every question (or even most of them). Give everyone the opportunity to participate. At the same time, don't put anyone on the spot—let subgroup members know they can pass on any question they're not comfortable answering.

3. Keep your subgroup time on track. There are suggested time limits for each section. Encourage good discussion, but don't be afraid to "rope 'em back in." If you do decide to spend extra time on a question or activity, consider skipping or spending less time on a later question or activity so you can stay on schedule.

CHILD CARE COORDINATOR

There are several ways you can approach the important issue of child care. Discuss as a group which alternative(s) you'll use:

1. The easiest approach may be for group members to each make their own child care arrangements. Some might prefer this; others may not be able to afford it on their own. If a parent or couple needs financial assistance, see if someone else in the group can help out in this area.

2. If your meeting area is conducive to it, have everyone bring their children to the meeting, and have on-site child care available so parents can pay on a child-by-child basis.

3. If most or all of your group members have young children, you could also consider rotating child care responsibilities around the group rather than paying someone else.

4. If there are members in your group with older children who are mature enough to watch the younger children, pay them to handle your child care. Maybe they can even do their own lesson. If so, Group offers a number of great materials for children of all ages—go to www.group.com to find out more.

5. Check to see if the youth group at your church would be interested in providing child care as a fundraiser.

It is wise to pre-screen any potential child care worker—paid or volunteer—who is watching children as part of a church-sanctioned activity (including a home Bible study). Your church may already have a screening process in place that can be utilized for your group. If not, Group's Church Volunteer Central network (www.churchvolunteercentral.com) is a great resource, containing ready-made background-check and parental-consent forms as well as articles and other online resources.